T0095811

Coffee Thoughts

Coffee Thoughts

REFLECTIONS FOR A PEACEFUL LIFE

David Dalton

iUniverse, Inc.
Bloomington

Coffee Thoughts
Reflections for a Peaceful Life

iUniverse books may be ordered through booksellers or by contacting:

iUniverse
1663 Liberty Drive
Bloomington, IN 47403
www.iuniverse.com
1-800-Authors (1-800-288-4677)

ISBN: 978-1-4759-4634-5 (sc)
ISBN: 978-1-4759-4636-9 (hc)
ISBN: 978-1-4759-4635-2 (ebk)

Library of Congress Control Number: 2012915861

Printed in the United States of America

iUniverse rev. date: 09/28/2012

"If I can but leave this life with a humble frame of mind, gentle thoughts toward others, a kind word, a noble deed, or a worthy thought imprinted upon the minds of others, then I will have accomplished a most notable feat, a value that will outlast the memory of my name."

David Dalton

The Author

Over his career as a pastor and educator, Dr. David Dalton has observed many of the life-inhibiting frames of thought one often holds that are detrimental to one's recovery and joy when walking through a crisis in life. He has witnessed countless individuals whose harmful attitudes have stolen enjoyment that should have been theirs to own.

It was not until David experienced his own personal tragedies of life, through an extreme and ongoing bout with life-threatening heart disease, that he became aware of the challenge one has in truly aligning his or her own personal attitudes into a synchronous system of wholesome attitudes for life and progress. This was, for David, a very personal journey. Along the way, he experienced the difficulty as well as the reward of adjusting attitudes better suited for his recovery and joy. Upon dealing with the pragmatics of his own potential death, he began discovering the truth about life. Encountering the "why" people respond as they do to life's experiences gave him the impetus to think through his own life's process and contemplate what constitutes a successful life in the first place.

Today, David spends his time as an educator and writer. He reflects on life through writing and service and enjoys it fully with his adult daughters, Olivia and Kristen, his grandchildren, Dalton and London, and his wife, Kaye. For David, life has never been such fun, even amid the inhibitions of health.

Dedication

Grandchildren are the light of one's life! I often think one has not truly lived, unless, upon having the opportunity to love a grandchild, one does not seize every occasion to enjoy and embrace the honor of grandparenthood. The large, beautiful dark eyes of my little granddaughter, London DeVizia, bring a relationship separated by distance, ever so close, transforming me into a person that I do not recognize, yet a person that I had always hoped I could be. Venues of modern technology like "Face Time" and other electronic means make little London's distant kisses so overwhelmingly close. It is as though all her love and emotion reaches right into the screen of her mother's iPhone, through cyberspace, to embrace all my passion and love for her on the screen of my iPad. I would not replace this time for any other time and will miss it when she "grows up." So now, while I have a chance to say it, and before this time passes, I want to convey the inexpressible joy over such real moments.

Contents

Introduction

The human thought cycle shifts in the course of a day between the things we see, the interactions we have, and the decisions we make. A host of other stimuli bear direct influence upon the outcome of our day. Choreographing our thoughts in the earlier part of our day may well tilt our thought cycle to our advantage, ultimately affecting the thoughts we think and the simultaneous actions accompanying them.

Some of these shifts of thought are well within the ranks of our control; yet, unforeseen circumstances, in some cases, intrude upon these expected courses of events. Retaining a consistent thought process, while around us circumstances shift dramatically, is the test of a healthy mind and spirit.

The power of one's thoughts bearing upon the structure of life cannot be overstated. Thoughts shape our reactions, tailor our responses, and contribute wholeness to our psychological well-being, while shaping our spiritual attributes and structuring our relational interactions.

While certainly not proclaiming to be a comprehensive manual on attitudinal wholeness, the pages ahead supply an opportunity for one to systematize their own thoughts. *Coffee Thoughts* introduces a series of general attitudes through which a single day can be shaped.

Now, if you are like me, almost all of us clamor for that private space, places where we can come aside from the usual; places exempt of demands, pressure, and distractions; a place that we can distinctively call "our own." For me, this place is really a creation of my own mind, seeing as the logistics are immaterial. This place, however, does always seem to involve a cup of coffee, some time that I have masterfully created for myself, and a space where I am clearly alone with my own thoughts; hence, the name *Coffee Thoughts*.

Using the Personal Coaching Questions

One of our greatest assets that is often deeply misunderstood and certainly underutilized is our innate human ability to assess our own attitudes and behaviors in some constructive way. This enables us to begin understanding our own mental function, or predictable patterns of response, and certainly our rational as well as our irrational behaviors. Some would refer to the mastery of interrelating successfully with one's inner self as a profound spiritual discovery. Others define it as their own version of the *human ethic of stewardship* over which we must take charge to experience a fulfilled and enhanced life. I find this exercise of self-assessment to be both profoundly spiritual and extremely responsible, certainly the highest ideal for tracking personal and relational standards across the board.

However, it is up to each person how he or she engages their own life in this pursuit. If we "know what is good for us," we will restrict our energies at changing personal behaviors to ourselves alone. This objective can be truly enhanced when, after successfully understanding ourselves, we offer some guiding help along the way to others who desire our input.

Self-coaching, as I will call it, is a venue toward establishing the parameters of personal sound judgment and thorough self-assessment. This form of self-coaching allows you, the person, to guide the process of introspection as deeply as you desire.

Immediately following each "Reflection" in *Coffee Thoughts*, you will find several "Personal Coaching Questions." This is a series of questions corresponding to the subject matter discussed in the "Reflection" that is intended to prompt and guide a self-assessment process. These questions posed are in no way intended to be comprehensive, nor are they intentioned to be fully exhaustive on any given subject matter. Instead, they are only as thorough as an individual wants to make them and as deeply assessing as one might desire to explore their own person. The technique merely launches the inquiry; however, if adequate reflective time is given to the process, the soul will open to deeply renewing capacities.

To make the most of the self-coaching process, honesty with oneself is critically important. Keeping a personal reflection journal is encouraged to serve as an alongside aide to the complete process of reflection and discovery. Be blessed and enjoy the process!

Coffee Thoughts

Reflection 1

Valuing Life's Simplicity

Valuing life's simplicity and enjoying the beauty of living it with ease is the ultimate objective now. Of course, this didn't come without a cost, to be sure. Living life by a different score card, I now no longer keep a running record of the number of people seen or the number of projects completed in the course of a day. Able to respond to daily events in a calm yet deliberate manner, the accomplishment of objectives has a more "caring tone" about them, enabling all remaining remnants of the former "living-on-the-edge" philosophy to die a long-awaited death. Once thinking my identity was based upon the number of appointments kept, now, life is reduced to the bare minimum and restructured in such a way as to enjoy the fruitful impact of every single accomplishment. I must admit, I would never have relinquished the "busy" for the "simple" voluntarily, and I cannot claim the credit for such realignment of life. I give the credit where credit is due. Health issues over which I had no control imposed this radical transformation of outlook upon me. Initially, reluctantly submissive to a realignment of life's values, I now thoroughly appreciate the imposed change, and embrace it as a healthy philosophy of life. Now, I am completely comfortable with my "new normal."

Personal Coaching Questions

Valuing Life's Simplicity

1. What goals can I list that contribute to the well-being of my sound mind and spirit?

2. In what ways have my schedule and way of life supported the nurturing of a calm disposition?

3. In what ways am I able to organize my current life system to simplify and relax anxieties?

Reflection 2

Reflecting Deeply

Reflecting deeply is similarly related to the breath of fresh air one draws immediately after breaking free from an area where a putrid smell dominates. Reflection is a gift, empowering the soul with a sigh of relief from the mere stagnancy of routine thoughts. Through the "incidences of life," as disconcerting as they might be and as wearing as they may be upon our soul, one can find new meaning, fresh perspective, and the impetus to forge ahead with renewed vision. New perspective comes as one contemplates life, even while encountering fallout from the present circumstances upon them. Living free in the "new thoughts of now" lifts the peril of present realities. As one continues to apply healthy reflection to the incidences encountered, thoughts develop and perspectives emerge, providing "a haven of refuge amid a torrent of difficulty." Inspiration comes through personal reflection, enabling the journey to have been worth the toil and the future to be far more promising than previously thought.

Personal Coaching Questions

Reflecting Deeply

1. In what ways are my current thoughts full of vision? In what ways do they imperil fresh and renewed vision for life?

2. In what ways do my perspectives need to change in order to encounter a new vision for life, my profession, faith, etc.?

3. How might I implement a new system of thought that will provide a "haven of refuge" amid even the most difficult circumstances?

Reflection 3

Observing the Colors in Variant Situations

Leaving Alabama on Tuesday, my ride was a therapeutic one as I could not keep my eyes off the changing leaf color of the beautiful autumn scenery. "Etched on the 'easel of creation' is God's graphic signature to be sure," I thought. Arriving in Orlando, driving through the city today to Florida Hospital for my heart tests, I was reminded of the dichotomy of variant scenes between northern Alabama's colors and the ones I observed in Orlando. Central Florida awaited me with green grass, beautiful lively trees, manicured landscapes and imaginative, colorful, and exotic blossoms. Walking the sidewalk to the hospital entrance, I encountered a lined corridor of blooming gardens. Once inside, apprehensions of the heart procedures awaiting me were left behind. Leaving the hospital following the procedure, I remembered many times through the years when I forfeited opportunities to see the beauty in difficult occasions. Beauty was always present, and color was constantly there; sadly, however, I failed to observe its distinction! So encompassed by the hardship, I missed the color! In retrospect, I "saw" the beauty, but failed to "observe" it, compromising my internal healing in the process!

Personal Coaching Questions

Observing the Colors of Variant Situations

1. When was the last time I paused to observe God's signature on the landscape and record the beauty observed?

2. In what way did I extract the fullest meaning out of the moment?

3. How might I describe the peace and tranquility experienced in the moments described?

4. If I were offered the opportunity to revisit the moment with the option to stay there for an extended period of time, how much time would I give to observing its beauty again?

5. What scenes would I note that I might have previously failed to observe?

6. What personal parameters would I put in place so I might enjoy the experiences of the future, allowing them the opportunity to radiate with fullest meaning and significance?

Reflection 4

Embracing the Situation

The "outcome" of the present situation is yet to be seen. The end result depends much upon my willingness to "embrace" the current state of things, even with all its present liabilities. Accepting the parameters as they are now is important to the shaping and development of my own attitude. My ownership of the situation invariably involves time and patience, virtues of which I often have less than needed. However, by my not becoming frustrated in the moment, I remain intentionally confident that it will all work out over time. The hope this position breeds enables me to live with this "new normal," while growing accustomed to the possibility that when the episode is completed, I will be different, and everyone involved will be more perfectly aligned with the purpose for which the situation, in all reality, came along in the first place. My greatest confidence comes from prayer that sooths my disposition. My assurance of God's involvement in this issue calms my anxieties and my prior need to control the outcome.

Personal Coaching Questions

Embracing the Situation

1. Seeing that the current situation requires much investment of my time and the involvement of my emotions, in what ways do I consider this investment of time worthwhile?

2. What components, if integrated, would create a more rewarding experience and enhance the outcome?

3. Emerging out of the situation, even amid its present encumbrances, what potential outcomes do I foresee?

4. In what ways do I propose to manage my current emotions to assure the most potential from the situation?

5. What approaches do I currently employ that tend to sooth my present disposition as I anticipate the most positive outcome from the situation?

Reflection 5

Managing Emotions

The "mixed bag" of emotions encountered in life constantly reminds us of our "mere humanity." The hemisphere of emotions experienced in these up-and-down times reveals the constant interaction between the thoughts inside our minds and the events outside us, affecting our physical, mental, and social selves. This constant pressure between the two generates a vacuum where essential management over our own faculties must take place in order to shore up and sustain soundness of mind. The tasks of managing our emotions are connected to the outcomes between our "initial thoughts" and our "final thoughts" regarding any given experience or challenge. The ease of management is measured by our willingness and ability to personally critique our errors while at the same time celebrating our growth since the last challenge. Hence, the keeping of a "measurable record" is one among many ways of managing our emotions while monitoring the reliability of our decision-making processes. Becoming comfortable with and trusting in our own internal "life management style," while displaying evenness in the process through which we execute our decisions, goes a long way in complementing our stability of mind and spirit.

Personal Coaching Questions

Managing Emotions

1. Assessing my current situation, what things present in my responses to the situation indicate my comfortableness with my own humanity?

2. Observing the process by which I personally manage my emotions, what points can I extract from this process that become indicators of my progress between my "beginning thoughts" and my "final thoughts" regarding a situation (for example, irritation versus calmness or anxiety versus serenity)?

3. Record these outcomes in my journal.

Reflection 6

Enjoying Companionship

The simple acts of human interaction are most intriguing to me these days. Last night at Wendy's was an elderly couple seemingly in their upper 80's. Standing side-by-side at the counter facing the cashier waiting patiently their turn, the lady ordered first as the cashier made eye contact with her. The budget meal consisted of a simple hamburger (on the dollar menu), and a small chocolate frosty. The cashier waited patiently with understanding and compassion at the lady's slowness to retrieve her change. Finding the amount, the lady moved slowly, shifting her feet, carefully placing her cane in a safe place to await her meal. The little man followed suit to order his meal. The cashier said, "$2.16." Again, in like fashion, finding two dollars, and commencing to count out sixteen pennies, the man proceeded slowly but surely to examine each penny one-by-one from his dainty change pouch. For the rest of the evening, my mind and eyes were fixed on the quality of their interaction during the brief moments my wife and I were there. Watching the couple conversing simply, smoothly, respectfully and peacefully, I assumed this to be their situation: "All alone, with former spouses deceased, they now sought companionship, proving this to be a most satisfying gift to one another."

Personal Coaching Questions

Enjoying Companionship

1. In what way does the beauty of companionship play a vital role in my emotional and social well-being?

2. How appreciative have I been of companionship and friendship when the opportunities present themselves?

3. What ways can I create a more conducive environment for encouraging companionship to thrive?

4. What barriers to friendship might I need to reform in order to make the experience mutually rewarding for the other participant?

5. What things do I have to offer in a relationship that will draw others toward me?

6. Classify some of the specifics of my current relationships that have proven to meet specific needs in my life.

7. In what ways, in my estimation, do the other parties in my current relationships experience mutual benefit from a relationship with me?

Reflection 7

Appreciating the Twilight Moments

Today had to have ranked high on God's creative calendar. Driving up the mountain toward home in northern Alabama, the preciseness of the time in the late afternoon coupled with the scenery of the mountainside brought the providence of the moment to bear on my internal thoughts. The evening sun, sinking behind the overcast clouds leaving a silhouette of fire bursting forth from behind them, combined with the bright golden, beautiful brown, and bountiful red autumn leaves covering the entire mountain scape, lit the scene with a spectacular radiance indescribable with human words. Before that precise moment, I was lamenting that the day was coming to a close, until . . . until I saw this autumn spectrum. The mere sight gave the impetus to process the beauty of "twilight moments." Twilight moments give us a gift like none other—brief providential moments of time, to capture the nature of the day at its pinnacle of expression. With the day fighting to remain alive and the night fast imposing its presence, the stark contrast between them reveals the power of this moment's "contemplative fervor." Capturing this pinnacle of expression is only for those, who, in the momentary window of time, hastily seize the moment that is so quickly fading.

Personal Coaching Questions

Appreciating the Twilight Moments

1. "Twilight moments" are those small windows of time between the close of one period, day, or time in our lives and the beginning of another! With that in mind, what is my approach to ascribing significance to the present closure of the chapter or period in my life?

2. What are the typical emotions I encounter when one life era seems to come to a close? Do I sense that another time is about to dawn, and with anticipation, look forward to the next journey? Or, do I encounter sadness and disparity, as if that which is familiar to me is now gone? Explain these emotions in further detail.

3. What are some of the "pinnacle of expression" moments that for me sum up the meaning and extravagance of this time now closing for me?

4. What precious memories might I bring forward into the new day dawning that will prove to be a source of enjoyment for me for some time to come?

Reflection 8

Learning to Trust

The opportunity to trust is never far from me. At the times when I finally "get my bearings" and become comfortable with the current "state of ease," another challenge seems to come along, calling into question my present easiness, propelling me toward another opportunity to trust God all the more. Seeing this as a normal progression for me, while it used to take "strong currents of resistance" to jolt me into the presence of God, now, mere "ripples on the pond of life" are enough to convince me to run toward God for even the smallest provisions. Anticipating opportunities to "perfect my trust," I now tend to recognize the very instant another "trust moment" emerges. Seeing all the parallels from previous experiences, I seize this moment to extract all the beauty I can from this opportunity to develop my trust in a more comprehensive way. With this internal mechanism present, I find that most situations possess the ability to "trigger my faith" in some beautiful way.

Personal Coaching Questions

Learning to Trust

1. What noticeable shifts have I observed in my reluctance or readiness to trust God's guidance and involvement in my future and life in recent days?

2. In what ways would I describe my capacity to trust God's involvement in the outcome of my circumstances in the here and now?

3. When an unfamiliar experience comes my way, what is my natural inclination at first glance of the approaching situation? Is it to trust God completely, to fear, to immediately begin to strategize the situation in my own mind, or some other response? Explain in further detail.

Reflection 9

Encountering "Invasions of Normality"

Life often takes us on journeys so unpredictable to the typical "order of things" in order to perfect in us the understanding of God's character, while placing us symmetrically in clearer proximity to His established and purposed plan for us. These "invasions of normality," while not often diminishing our questioning the "whys" of their happenings, do, in time with introspection, lead us more definitively to our conclusion of the "rightness of God's decisions." Assessing the meaning and benefits of such excursions from "the normal," while justifying the extra time spent on the journey, is, in the end, the ultimate objective of our living and evaluating these experiences! In truth, in the aftermath of it all, it can be said, "The journey has been well worth the time spent, and the value has far outweighed the inhibitions experienced by the inconveniences."

Personal Coaching Questions

Encountering "Invasions of Normality"

1. When anything out of the ordinary or beyond the reach of "typical" happenings enters my sphere of experience, what is my usual response? Does it catch me by surprise? Does it unsettle my emotions? What other responses do I encounter?

2. What best describes my initial response to these "beyond the ordinary" intrusions?

3. What is my more graduated response after a time of contemplating these "invasions of normality?"

4. Does contemplation normalize the situation, bringing relevance and rationalization to my understanding of the situation?

5. Between the time of my initial response and my graduated (or more collected) response, what do I discover about myself?

Reflection 10

Discovering Beauty in Life's Contrasts

Every day life offers us many options and hands us an opportunity to view it in a distinct way. Choices are made, usually in an instant, which determine that day's value to us. The placement of these distinct happenings in the entire "schematic of our life" determines the perspective we have toward them. What we see as the backdrop or in the foreground, or what we choose to mentally exclude from the picture altogether, or even those happenings we decide to contrast against one another either skews, informs, or shapes life's meaning for us. The haste with which we often attribute meaning to a particular life happening often contributes to the undervaluing of that event in its overall placement in the scope of our life. Contemplation powerfully affords us the opportunity to clearly and comprehensively assess the value of each moment and makes the difference in our "extracting the nectar" out of life or merely "buzzing around." Traveling down a major highway this week observing the busyness of commerce in contrast to the beautiful wild flowers adorning the shoulders of the roadway afforded me this lesson. The passing trucks failed to inhibit the beautiful colors of the flowers as I stopped to observe the view from the shoulder of the road.

Personal Coaching Questions

Discovering Beauty in Life's Contrasts

1. How quickly do I notice the contrasts of life?

2. Do I sense these contrasts as having a voice of their own to speak to me in the moment?

3. Is most of life merely "customary," or do I notice the stark contrasts in culture, expression, and dimensions daily encountered?

4. Amid these contrasts, in what way do I intentionally stop to contemplate and assess these life contrasts, extracting the fullest beauty out of the routine around me?

5. What things might I implement in order to gain a more complete experience and fuller meaning from the contrasts of life?

Reflection 11

Exhibiting Grace Toward Others

"Grace" is that "gentleness of spirit" we afford to others when they do not possess the same opinions we hold. When apportioned amply, grace softens the most deliberate and opposing mind, while revealing and even relaxing our own obstinate opinions as well. Grace truly possesses a very "dual nature." Indeed, grace is such a gentle term, yet when introduced into the most contentious situations causes an otherwise "alarmed spirit" to be quieted, making a peaceful resolve ultimately possible. Likewise, graceful people possess an inner resolve, producing the absence of contention, ultimately contributing to inner and corporate harmony. Graceful people are models for all of our human interactions. Even as I sit this morning, I think of a few individuals whose grace shown toward me has caused my thoughts to turn this direction.

Personal Coaching Questions

Exhibiting Grace
Toward Others

1. What recent incidences can I point to where an attribute of grace displayed toward others changed the environment, enabling dialogue to open between two opposing opinions?

2. What situations can I describe where a deeper expression of grace toward others involved would have had a potentially different effect upon the outcome of the situation?

3. Observing my current spirit, to what degree would I describe myself as a person who is full of grace toward others?

4. What plans can I currently make to enhance my own display of grace toward others?

Reflection 12

Applying Stewardship Over Current Opportunities

Before moving ahead with fresh vision for one's life, family, organization, or interests, becoming a truly honorable steward of present opportunities is the first criteria to be accomplished. Applying one's mind to "making meaning" of the current prospects is responsible stewardship to say the least. Possessing a genuine openness to ask deeply probing questions regarding one's current situation ultimately leads to an honest "truth bearing of soul and mind." While truth at this level penetrates one's comfort zones, it also supplies the integrity necessary to integrate a system of true stewardship into one's life and throughout one's opportunities, present and future. This accomplishment, achieved in even the most seemingly insignificant spheres of one's life, serves well to establish healthy prospects for future opportunities.

Personal Coaching Questions

Applying Stewardship Over Current Opportunities

1. Upon evaluating my personal management over present opportunities, how would I describe myself if asked, "In what way am I a faithful steward over all of my present opportunities?"

2. In what ways do I hold myself to higher standards than I apply to others in regards to appreciating and managing my current holdings, responsibilities, and talents?

Reflection 13

Displaying a "Christ Grace" Toward Others

When others disappoint me, ultimately displaying less than courteous attitudes toward me, or when they show their "human nature" more abundantly than I can seemingly bear at the time, I choose to display "grace" toward them in these times that test the very character of my own identity. This measures the memory, or lack thereof, of Christ's own attitude toward me, when I, like they, displayed similar harshness toward others. Understanding this "Christ Grace" so adequately preserves me from the unnecessary spirit of irritability, retaliation, intolerance, and offense so typical of me in the times I conveniently forget Christ's own grace toward me. Christ's Grace is the "reminder of my own full story," a story so easily forgotten when I fail to exhibit grace toward others as I should.

Personal Coaching Questions

Displaying a "Christ Grace" Toward Others

1. In what ways do I seek to afford others the latitude to be "fully human" without holding them rigidly liable for their own errors?

2. When irritated, or even tempted to retaliate, what efforts do I make to quickly squelch the ferocity of my emotions?

3. What actions in others invoke my own personal irritabilities? What intolerances toward other's positions do I display? In what ways am I willing or unwilling to dialogue about differences?

4. What forms of retaliation am I contemplating at present?

5. Describe some instances where I have had a "less than gracious reaction" toward another person.

6. In those moments, what were my own thoughts about God's grace toward me? Do I hold these thoughts of God's grace dear to me, or do I discard them in the heat of the moment, merely reacting out of raw emotion?

Reflection 14

Appreciating Trusted Friendship

The discouragement of recent days, struggling with my own attitudes toward the adjustments I am making in the journey back to recovery of health, has been bearable due to the strength of a trusted friend. Trusting them with my life's issues has given me a venue through which I can "come clean" with the many personal struggles and attitudes so disconcerting to my spirit now. Finding an understanding ear, as they have displayed, has restored my faith in others. I have found that we need not have many friends to have a satisfying life, but just a few with whom we can feel thoroughly comfortable sharing our most inward thoughts. Friends of this nature give us the impetus we need to value the depth friendship affords once again.

Personal Coaching Questions

Appreciating Trusted Friendship

1. What undue expectations do I place upon current relationships?

2. In what ways do my expectations enhance or diminish my current relationship qualities?

3. What criteria are in place for the development of close friendships in my life?

4. Is there a mutuality that emerges within my friendships? Is there an equal and derived benefit for all participants involved?

5. At what level do I share my inward thoughts with others openly and without reservation?

6. What are my current levels of comfort within my relationships?

Reflection 15

Guarding a "Sacred Trust"

"Sacred Trust" are the words I ponder today. "Sacred" is that which is so highly valued that I would not on my life violate it. "Trust" is that which is held in safe keeping so no other person may exploit it. My "Sacred Trust" is that very delicate work between God and me; a work that I dare not share with others who may have the propensity to talk casually concerning what is very dear between my Lord and me. Renewing the sacred value of such an inward work in my life gives me the inspiration needed to desire an even deeper work in my relationship with God. Relationship with God becomes my most desired hope, finding that I can truly trust Him with even the deepest secrets of my heart. He, likewise, will hold that confidence so deeply within His own heart. This sacred bond between us ever reminds me of the value this relationship holds for me.

Personal Coaching Questions

Guarding a "Sacred Trust"

1. Seeing as "Sacred Trusts" are vital to my relationship with God, at what level do I see my "Sacred Trust" with God lacking?

2. At what level do I see growth forthcoming in this area?

3. What story do my "Sacred Trust" values tell about my faith?

4. What are some of my "Sacred Trusts?"

5. What does this discussion on "Sacred Trust" convey about my relationship with God?

Reflection 16

Encountering Moments of Solitude

Encountering the extremities of a severe heart condition, coupled with other personal challenges, forced into obscurity and isolation, weakened in body, and entrapped in my condition, my will still remains strong. It is in this place that I learn the role solitude plays. Only the intrusion of sickness could have gotten my attention in this way, as invasive as it is. At this time, I am learning to dance with a grace only silence brings. These moments of solitude have become a most desired state of mind since it is there that I discover the most precious gift of all—communion with Christ. These moments of silence are becoming to me the grace of renewal so deeply needed and presently enjoyed in my life.

Personal Coaching Questions

Encountering Moments of Solitude

1. In what ways do I find myself interacting with moments of silence, especially amid difficult times when I truly feel alone?

2. Are these moments of silence representative of God's approval or disapproval of my life or conduct? Explain.

3. At what point do I observe these moments of silence becoming true solitude, where peace with God is realized and His presence actualized in the moment?

4. What does this solitude prompt me to do in my present situation?

5. Am I comfortable with myself and with my relationship with God at the end of this moment of solitude?

6. What is my comprehensive take on these moments overall?

Reflection 17

Enjoying the Liberated Life

Seldom was Christ abrupt with anyone, except on those rare occasions when the "religious critics," whom He realized had no interest in His message in the first place, tried to entrap His good intentions. Christ's strategy when dealing with others clearly consisted of conversational-toned dialogue. He, to say the least, was thoroughly gentle, except on those rare occasions when His abruptness provided the jolt needed to make a clear point of His objections to outlandish actions. Interested in the individual's well-being, Christ provided the model for our interactions with others. He drew the person out to truthfully talk about his or her own situation of life, and then, coaching them to "come to terms with their reality," He encouraged them to appreciate their freedom from condemnation of the past. In the case of the woman in John 8:9-11, Christ made it very clear that He did not condemn her for her past, nor should she continue to live repressively enslaved to her former way of life, and neither should she live under the repression of other's feelings about her. Instead, she should now go on to live a wholesome and liberated life that He so graciously gave her permission to enjoy.

Personal Coaching Questions

Enjoying the Liberated Life

1. In what ways have I recently come to terms with my own failures without being totally destroyed by them?

2. Not designed to bear condemnation over our own failures, in what ways have I personally embraced the liberation afforded me through Christ's words in John 8:9-11?

3. Draw from this Biblical story the significance of permission granted by Christ to enjoy a liberated life.

4. How might I balance a liberated life with personal responsibilities for my own conduct?

5. What does true liberation from guilt mean to me personally?

Reflection 18

Examining the Motives
for Serving Christ

My thoughts were drawn to the story of the rich man and Lazarus recorded in Luke16:19-31. I questioned, "Would I still serve Christ, if indeed I, like the rich man, were already destined to spend eternity apart from God? And then, would I be concerned for my brothers and friends if any personal incentive for me to go to heaven no longer existed? Would I care about where my friends or family go after they die, since my fate had already been sealed?" Answering these questions may indeed reveal much about our personal motives of why we follow Christ in the first place. I mean, "Would I truly serve Christ even if the incentive of Heaven was left out?" After answering these questions in my own mind today, I confirmed that I would serve Christ no matter my final destiny, and I would still do all that I could to "warn" my friends of impending perils of not following Christ themselves. With that confirmed in my mind and with the standing assurance of heaven still in view, should I not all the more hastily care for my friends and family by sharing my love and passion for Christ here and now?

Personal Coaching Questions

Examining the Motives
for Serving Christ

1. In what ways have I tested my own motives for serving Christ?

2. In what ways do I evaluate my own integrity regarding intentions and motives toward my service of Christ, and for that matter, service to others?

3. Is my heart pure enough in my love toward Christ that if no personal incentives benefitting me existed, would I continue to follow Christ?

4. What responsibility do I bear for sharing my motives for serving Christ with others?

Reflection 19

Rediscovering One's Gifts

How does one bounce back from isolation and loss into a place of internal significance and personal resolve? It was as if I heard a voice say, "Rediscover your gifts that have become lost in the shuffle of your experience! Those gifts that have taken new shape amid your challenges now need to be redefined. Upon searching and finding those new abilities emerging from the experiences you have had, there you will find the 'new you.' Your gifts have not diminished with your calamity; they have only matured to a greater potential for expression." I must admit, I do not tend to carry on this type of dialogue within myself, but this time, it seemed divinely legitimate and altogether appropriate. With this word, I realized, gifts given to us by God most often come to us initially in "raw form." The beauty of our rediscovery of these latent gifts is wrapped up in the excitement generated in the find. Usually following the graphic loss of a job, finances, career, health, and in some cases family as well, the ability of one to see hope amid the clouds appears insurmountable at the time. Rediscovery of those lost gifts plays a definitive role in the emergence of the renewed self, a place where one finds the "image of God" who indelibly stamped His face upon our own in the first place. The richness of our future potential accompanies this thrilling rediscovery of our gifts.

Personal Coaching Questions

Rediscovering One's Gifts

1. What significant life-altering experience have I encountered that has played a significant role in either the diffusing of my own gifts and talent potential or the enhancing and expansion of it?

2. When was there a time that my exuberance for life prompted my desire and birthed healthy feelings of personal significance and potential contribution?

3. In what ways have my experiences, as detrimental as they have been to my own feelings of self worth, contributed to a potential redefining of previous gifts and talents I once held so dear?

Reflection 20

Finding Appreciation in Lack

Nothing causes me to rediscover my appreciation for something more than finding myself in lack of it. My thoughts are germane to the absence of what I once thought would be a lifelong career. During my long and extensive battle with sickness and other personal issues, my appreciation now for the opportunities I once possessed is renewed. Those prospects are again returning in limited dimension, and I will always be aware of the time when they were completely absent.

Personal Coaching Questions

Finding Appreciation in Lack

1. What are some things I once enjoyed that I now find myself in lack of? (For example, health, wealth, career, relationships, etc.)

2. What role did these things once play in the composite whole of my identity, personhood, and well-being?

3. What things have I lost in times past that I now have a healthy appreciation for? Do I now experience a balance between my desire and my need?

Reflection 21

Gaining Inspiration from a Personal Friend

Moments when the pain of life dragging behind me is overwhelmingly disproportionate to the size of my shoulders, I am deeply inspired by a personal friend who has carried his hurt and pain proportionately well. This friend of mine has a trait that inspires me daily since knowing him and his story. Having been judged by the story others were free to tell about him, when having the opportunity to "set the record straight" and exonerate himself, I have watched him remain silent to avoid drawing harm to his accusers. "Thanks friend. Your life and response speak volumes to me! I trust I can follow your example when misjudged in the same manner!"

Personal Coaching Questions

Gaining Inspiration from a Personal Friend

1. When I encounter extensive pain, is there a person that I can look to who represents a real example of one who has carried their pain well in life?

2. Imagine for a moment the degrees of an individual's pain, hurt, and loss. Thinking through the venue of their life, ask the question, "What lessons in the way they have carried themselves amid their dilemma might I also list as definitive lessons for my own and current struggle?"

3. In what ways might I express my own appreciation to that individual for their notable example and inspiration given to me?

Reflection 22

Establishing a Safe Philosophy of Life

Last night, I typed my four-fold philosophy toward life! I would like to say that I have adhered to these all of my life; however, that is not the case, and the fallout for not doing so has been extreme! (1) I accept life as it comes, without complaint, assuming that within the hardship of the situation, the signature of God is stamped upon it! (2) I embrace all the parameters of the situation as they now are without becoming emotionally embattled. (3) I do my best to clean up the mess and make sense out of the rubble after the dust settles, and I will consequently not try to circumvent God's involvement in the situation, especially as I perceive His lessons clearly identified. (4) I will first judge myself by the judgments I am tempted to levy against others, and if, when accomplishing that, there is any room left for judging others, then I will afford to that person the latitude to be fully human.

Personal Coaching Questions

Establishing a Safe Philosophy of Life

1. Assuming it is a healthy experience for us all to chart personal philosophies for living our lives, by appropriating specific reflection time to write in our journal, ask yourself the following question, "What can I reasonably say are the personal philosophies I hold in life that are non-negotiable, despite shifting experiences?" List them.

2. In what ways will I apply my best intention to hold to these standards even amid challenges and the changing culture?

Reflection 23

Experiencing God's Presence in Trouble

II Corinthians 1:4-5 helps me make sense out of the insensible events of life. Holding onto the hope that "encumbering events" will one day burst forth with meaning and resound with possibility, I worked hard, against all the odds of my human nature, to correct my attitudes toward them. Realizing that the presence of God resided in my troubles, I knew that when my spirit was right, the fog would be removed, and I would see the providential meaning of these distressing events with all clarity. At that time, I then obtained my own voice to speak to others, encouraging them with the same reassuring words I had received from the experience. Understanding that suffering has everything to do with my coming to terms with myself, my identity with Christ's suffering, and my connection with others makes the "period of trouble" bearable.

Personal Coaching Questions

Experiencing God's Presence in Trouble

1. How can I connect the scripture in II Corinthians 1:4-5 to a current difficulty in my own life? What personal parallels can I draw between this scripture and my situation?

2. What outcome can I see in this current struggle?

3. What sense can I make, even now, out of this difficulty?

4. What role does my attitude play in the formation of meaning in this situation?

5. Do I envision my own voice taking shape, enabling me to encourage others and speak into their lives amid their trouble?

6. What can I identify as some of the potential possibilities regarding the composite whole of my life coming out of this dilemma?

Reflection 24

Finding Meaning in the Absence of God's Voice

I realize that God chooses not to speak to me tonight in the way I am so accustomed to hearing His voice in my thoughts. "God, of all times in my life, I really need to hear YOU speak to me definitively tonight. I MUST hear your voice," I pleaded. In recent months I have found so serene, so calming to my mind, a gentle thought or an "abstract word" that becomes the seed for further contemplation. But not tonight! Not a single word! I mean, God always speaks to me in "words," sometimes in riddles, and then I seek to unpack the meaning; but God has never, I thought, spoken to me profoundly through the absence of His voice. Then it occurred to me to ask, "Is there a thought from HIS mind that I might glean in the absence of HIS words?" "Quietness! Stillness! The inactivity of God! What is it saying to me?" Then, the "thoughts of nothingness" and the feelings of isolation gave birth to tears, and through these tears, God speaks in this "venue of unfamiliarity." He is conveying to me that I do not necessarily need His voice or even His words when I have His presence, so profoundly real. I will not discount His silence, for within the quietness I profoundly encountered His personal presence.

Personal Coaching Questions

Finding Meaning in the Absence of God's Voice

1. Making an effort to describe my personal experience at a time when God's voice seemed so silent, what thoughts come to mind when speaking of those moments?

2. What do I remember regarding the emotion of my soul at the time?

3. When encountering God's silence for the first time in my recollection, what was my first inclination of thought?

4. In what way does God most often speak to me? Are there differences noted in the way God sometimes chooses to speak to me? If so, in what way does God speak in these times?

5. What are my manners of reception to His voice in my life? Describe this.

Reflection 25

Relinquishing the "What Could Have Been" Mindset

There are points where I could easily live in the "what could have been" mode, but that would be of little benefit in the here and now. While I certainly have room to evaluate my mistakes of the past, I look to God's redemptive future in the here and now. And, the here and now is reflectively sweet with the mercies and graces of God, with each day full of new surprise. With this mindset, I look to each day before me as holding ample supply needed for that day alone. Held within each single day is all the capacity from which I might extract the nectar needed for the particular moment of time.

Personal Coaching Questions

Relinquishing the "What Could Have Been" Mindset

1. In what ways do I live in the sphere of my past? Or, in what ways do I live liberated from my past failures?

2. What mechanisms do I have in place for deriving meaning from my past mistakes without remaining crippled by them?

3. What is my take on the here and now? How do I view my current potential?

4. What value do I assess to my present circumstances? What methods do I utilize in bringing this current value to bear on my future prospects?

Reflection 26

Experiencing a Liberating Grace

A person who professes forgiveness of their own sin through Christ's death on the cross yet purposefully and deliberately disdains a brother or sister, holding them rigidly liable for their human failings, sorely compromises the power of God's grace in the present. The "liberation of Grace" does not fully come to a person until they readily dismantle their offenses against others, relinquishing others from all liability and personal accountability for their perpetrating offenses. Upon learning the power of Grace's liberation, a person is free to embrace their brother or sister in the same way Christ embraces them. With this in mind, I now release myself from the chains of offense toward others by giving them the thorough latitude to be fully human. This results in my continuing to appreciate their human contribution without holding them to a standard that I myself cannot keep.

Personal Coaching Questions

Experiencing a Liberating Grace

1. What is my personal approach for dealing with the shortcomings and failures of others?

2. In what way do I seek to equalize my dealings between what I expect of myself and what I expect of others?

3. In what way do I minimize my weaknesses while concurrently magnifying the failures of others?

4. What remaining offenses toward others do I need to thoroughly work through?

5. How relevant to my situation do I see Colossians 3:17, where we are encouraged to give others latitude to fully express their humanity?

6. What does the term "forgiveness" mean to me?

Reflection 27

Adopting a Healthy "Mental Self-Talk"

Encouraging us to engage in healthy collaboration between our mind and our spirit, the scriptures declare that our most valued resource is often underutilized. Our thoughts are truly instrumental in shaping our mental, social, and spiritual well-being. During the times when we do not feel as if things will improve with our situation, the scriptures encourage us "to think on things that are pure, honest, lovely, and of good report." So, I surmise that the emotion over what I feel, what others say about me, or even what I am anxious about, can be harnessed, and I can honestly "talk myself into having a great day."

Personal Coaching Questions

Adopting a Healthy
"Mental Self-Talk"

1. When encountering a challenge to my mental, social, or spiritual well-being, what strategies do I utilize to talk myself through the encounter?

2. In what ways do the strategies I incorporate into "self-talk" contribute to better self-awareness, a more peaceful disposition, and ultimately, a more consistent self-image?

3. What role does the commitment to think higher, more productive thoughts, play in the general uplift of my body and soul?

Reflection 28

Admitting Weaknesses

Becoming comfortable with our weaknesses is not the liability one would suppose. Instead, it is truly an admirable strength. While disclosing our human frailty produces a particular discomfort, a special grace is given to the "humble of heart." We display our strength when we expose our weaknesses. In that state of mind, we identify with the weakened Christ of the cross, who, hanging vulnerable and exposed, opened His arms to a hurting and disenfranchised world that has, over these many centuries, felt comfortably safe in His care. Our human transparency is a beautiful expression of our identity with a suffering Christ and a remarkable beginning to a real identity with hurting people.

Personal Coaching Questions

Admitting Weaknesses

1. How do I look at my weaknesses? Do I tend to compartmentalize them away from the viewing public and even from my own mind?

2. In what ways do I discuss my weaknesses without feelings of intimidation or the undervaluing of my personal self-worth?

3. In what ways do I conceal my weaknesses?

4. In what way does the picture of the "vulnerable Christ of suffering" identify with my own weaknesses?

5. What ways and means might I utilize in ministering to others through my weaknesses?

Reflection 29

Finding New Meaning in Former Thoughts

The scriptures never cease to amaze me! Like many people, I have the luxury of numerous Bibles at my disposal, using different versions for varying points of interest. This weekend, I picked up a Bible I used about a year ago during a troubling time in my life. While rereading the passage I had marked the year earlier, I recalled the emotion amid the "crux of struggle" and the meaning contained in my remarks written beside a Colossian passage. Remembering the precise incidents and feelings of a year ago, I reread the passage again this weekend with the hindsight of the experiences of that time. This has resulted in the passage becoming more deeply personal and more insightfully alive. So, while my experiences do not dictate my theology, they certainly do supply freshness to my understanding of the scriptures.

Personal Coaching Questions

Finding New Meaning in Former Thoughts

1. What scriptures might I identify that were meaningful to me at a previous time asking, "What new insights emerge from these scriptures now?"

2. As I write these new insights in my journal and compare them to previous ones, how do I measure the differentials? The distance between previous thinking and present thinking are indicators of one's growth during two epochs of time. Describe this "growth of thought" differential.

3. In what ways has my experience in recent days contributed to the new understanding I have of this passage of scripture?

4. Chart this progress over a period of time.

Reflection 30

Legitimizing Other's Humanity

It helped me adjust my responses toward others when I discovered an approach suggested by Paul the Apostle in dealing with human relationships. Addressing the Colossian church in his epistle, Paul encouraged them to give others the space to express their fullest humanity without internalizing the conduct of others as a personal offense. Adhering to this philosophy does not prevent my noticing another's actions, as Paul asserts, but I have found it does assist in managing the personal or corporate liability their actions levy on the whole of those involved. The more I am able to release the thought of another's infraction from my spirit, the more potential I have for preventing additional hurt to myself and the corporate group. In actuality, this approach increases my chances for becoming a "healer" to the situation and not merely a "wounded bystander." Hence, the "hurting people hurt people" cycle is prevented from being passed on, potentially remediating the situation towards a good outcome.

Personal Coaching Questions

Legitimizing Other's Humanity

1. Seeing as we are "human," and from time to time, we all "act our nature," what objectives have I set for dealing with these "human" occurrences in others when they arise?

2. Are there areas within my own interactions where I observe this duplicitous nature, the "image of man" and the "image of God," conflicting with each other for the upper hand?

3. Name specific biblical characters who struggled to correct this conflict. Identify incidences in Jesus' life where He demonstrated for us how to successfully integrate and at times moderated between the two natures without conflict.

4. In what way do I personally struggle with my behaviors being offensive to others?

5. In what way do I embrace a "release and let go" philosophy toward potential offenses of others toward me?

Reflection 31

Learning to Cry Again

"What is going on in the minds of these children?" I wondered. I was confused since I did not read in their eyes the typical selfishness, anger, or resentment one might expect of children in their dilemma. I mean, I would have expected these small children to be filled with great degrees of psychological and behavioral dysfunction. But I saw none! They loved so deeply, hugged so tightly, clung ever so strongly, as if they understood human emotion more than me. They looked into my eyes as if to peer past my pain and into the center of my soul, reading my mind with such accuracy while saying, "It truly is ok for you to have the thoughts you have about us!" While captivating my mind and simultaneously grabbing my affection, they held my heart safely within their hands so gently, speaking into it with convincing voices. I realized, fighting back the tears, that these children had breached the veneer of my soul and had entered a tender place in my heart. Versed in their conditions before I arrived, I was already braced for interacting with "distant precaution." But then, I held them in my arms, their fevered bodies burning my skin. These beautiful children are all HIV positive, having contracted AIDS from their mothers who are prostitutes on the streets of Mumbai, India. Thanks children of the *Jubilee Home of Project Rescue* for teaching me to cry again.

Personal Coaching Questions

Learning to Cry Again

1. Specifying particular moments where an interaction with someone melted my heart, what can I describe about those moments by recreating the particulars, including the emotion, the thoughts, and the recollected responses of thought in the following days?

2. What about those moments would I desire to live again in order to experience the warmth of compassion? What vulnerabilities of emotion at that moment, do I, in hindsight, see as a valuable or desired disposition?

3. In my quest to live a valuably significant life, what things can I do in the days or months ahead that will potentially renew and affirm my quest for life's meaning?

Reflection 32

Becoming Comfortable
With My Humanity

I am so liberated to know that I now have the freedom to talk about my failures, exposing my own vulnerabilities to others, while not alarmed with those who might feel compelled to take advantage of my weaknesses in the process. Upon discovering the strength blatant honesty with myself brings me, I realized how I longed to reach this place. Now being there, I no longer feel embarrassed by my failures or by talking about them freely, and am perfectly grateful for these "less than desirable episodes of my personal history," seeing as they have now truly become a remarkable story of formation and grace for me. This freedom provides me the internal substance to relax and enjoy my life without feeling the compulsion to perform beyond what is reasonably expected.

Personal Coaching Questions

Becoming Comfortable With My Humanity

1. Do I have difficulty talking about my mistakes and failures? If so, why does this difficulty exist? Is fear over the exposure of my own vulnerabilities a factor? Or, are there other issues such as the fear of the exploitation of my weaknesses that are worth considering?

2. How do I truly view myself? Do I view my failures as defining my character? If so, in what way? Do I see my mistakes as inhibiting my future? If so, in what way?

3. In all reality, is the fact of my own humanity problematic for me? If so, in what way? Do I feel that I give myself respectful room to be thoroughly human?

4. What steps might I take to clear the way for a productive resolution to this issue? List the steps in detail I might take.

Reflection 33

Expressing the Beauty of Today

This is such a beautiful morning! Sitting in my flower garden, with a cup of coffee (of course), observing the new blooms and enjoying the beauty of life while listening intently to an array of birds echoing against the backdrop of this cool mountain air, I find myself thinking, "Is this not one of nature's most beautifully expressive mornings!" Suddenly, I notice in the moment that my field of view enlarges greatly as I stop to hear the sounds and ponder the happenings around me. Suddenly, I begin hearing the birds in a different way with each variety's distinct music and their blending melodies standing out on their own. In many ways, this moment parallels an array of experiences I have daily since I have committed to the "refreshed way of life," where every moment and every sound has a distinct echo of its own. My life is daily filled with the most promising options; options to see, observe and experience everything around me in just about any way that I choose to see them, finding my joy not in the "happening" itself but within the choice I make in the given moment to "take it all in." The reason I know that this day will be as enjoyable, if not more so than yesterday, is due to the attitude I possess toward it already.

Personal Coaching Questions

Expressing the Beauty of Today

1. Do I honestly possess the kind of reflection time that contributes to soundness of mind and life? Do I intentionally create the time and coordinate the places where contemplation inspires me toward creativity of mind?

2. If my opportunities for contemplation and meditation expand, how might my outlook toward life expand with them?

3. In considering my life now, what descriptive words would I use to adequately reflect the nature and state of my life? (Attempt to use as many descriptive words as possible in self-reflection and observation.)

Reflection 34

Experiencing Internal Satisfaction

I asked myself the question this morning, "What could be better than this life I'm living?" Now there are a number of things I could be doing today that would be enjoyable like seeing my daughters and grandkids, or visiting one of the places on my "bucket list" with my wife, or a host of other life-enriching experiences. But, while any of these or other experiences can be thoroughly enjoyable and honoring of the commitments I have made to myself, that which puts them on the map of "sheer and indescribable satisfaction" is the ongoing "inner rest of my soul" I experience. Being so fully complete on the inside qualifies the external experiences to be mutually enjoyed. Hence, I am relishing the memory of a recent trip as I savor a cup of hot Turkish tea.

Personal Coaching Questions

Experiencing Internal Satisfaction

1. Thinking back in life, is there an earlier point where I more thoroughly enjoyed my coffee or tea time? If so, what prevents my thorough enjoyment of these times now?

2. Describing my frame of mind during this allotted time, what goes on in my thinking that contributes to the making of this time "exclusively mine?"

3. Would I consider visiting a country like Turkey? If so, when would I like to go? If not, then why not? Where else would I love to visit and why?

4. Have I ever experienced any "Turkish Tea moments" where I interacted with a culture and savored its delicacies? If so, when sitting down to enjoy this treat, in what ways, in those moments, did I take the time to savor the culture in my thoughts? Record some reflections remembered about that time. How could I have made this experience even richer?

Reflection 35

Exhibiting Faith Amid Life's Challenges

Faith finds its best expression and ultimately is greatly measured for us when, against the odds of some "life challenge," we refuse to lose hope even amid horribly painful circumstances. Between the tensions of discomfort and hope for better, we find the passion to believe and press on, enduring well past that which would prevent us from otherwise obtaining the prize altogether. With this in mind, I resolve to draw from the present discomfort that which is woven into the moment, the courage to face all things encountered with an internal energy inside me, and optimism from beyond me. "I press toward a fulfilling future . . . ." (Philippians 3:14)

Personal Coaching Questions

Exhibiting Faith Amid Life's Challenges

1. What are some of my first responses amid a life challenge of some sort? Explaining my initial responses in detail, in what ways might I more successfully integrate a "faith response?"

2. Do challenging situations tend to shake my emotions, disconcert me, anger me, or invite me into the "center of my soul?" In what ways might I improve my initial responses?

3. Is there an internal mechanism that causes me to anticipate what is to come even amid the discomfort, and in what way is this present?

4. Do I have a general expectation that all things will work out for a good outcome? If so, list some general expectations regarding challenging situations I often encounter.

Reflection 36

Broadening My Selection of Friends

The people I want to befriend are those who are not necessarily devoid of conflict. Those who have had difficulty in their lives and have thoroughly and personally scrutinized their attitudes toward it often have something to say to me that will keep my feet from error. While many ostracize individuals with a "tainted past," often dismissing their story as not possessing any credible voice, I have learned otherwise that these individuals speak into my life with great wisdom and resolute thought, often formulating meaning from life experience that is profoundly different from the status quo. Creating an environment of hope, they recognize the value that their story brings to others and do not seek to live their lives away from people to whom they may deposit wonderful help and value. Determining to broaden my circle of friends, I am finding much delight in the enlarging possibilities.

Personal Coaching Questions

Broadening My Selection of Friends

1. Is there a current list of individuals from whom I have extracted the nectar of their life experiences? If so, who are they? In what ways might I open myself up to this wonderful world of value brought to my life through others?

2. Who in the past has affected my life positively? What was the story they told or the experiences they shared that contribute value to my life now?

3. What were the lessons they taught me that had a dramatic effect upon me or evoked some change within me?

Reflection 37

Ascribing Meaning to Life Happenings

Life happenings remain mere casual incidences until the time we ascribe meaning to them. With that inscription, the value of these experiences rises to the level of significance for our personal life and history. At that time, they contribute to the bank of memorable stories that make our life a truly better one to live. Bearing the stamp of God's providence, we then see these "accidental occurrences" or "interruptions of life" as backdrops to the larger purpose God has for us. Our greatest challenge is to observe these situations as bringing meaningful purpose for our instruction, our correction, or our future direction.

Personal Coaching Questions

Ascribing Meaning to
Life Happenings

1. What is my first inclination upon seeing a particular event happening in my life? Do I immediately identify the meaning in this happening?

2. Have I watched events transition in value as I stopped to ascribe meaning to the situation? How does making meaning out of instances in my life shape my entire frame of experience?

3. What is my perspective toward the "providence of God?" Do I see things that happen as possessing some providential purpose?

Reflection 38

Developing the
Art of Friendship

Thoroughly enjoying breakfast with a dear friend today reminds me of the sentiment Paul the Apostle had as he recollected his thoughts regarding his own friends in the city of Philippi. Having adopted a pattern of prayer for them in Philippians 1:3-6, sequentially and regularly appreciating their camaraderie as fellow "sharers of the work," he validates the present involvement of God in their lives as fresh and comprehensively moving toward complete perfection. With that in mind, as I step into an era of my life where the beauty of friendship now enhances my daily thoughts, I am inspired to "raise the bar of expectation," keeping the kind of friends around me that renew my confidence in the art of friendship and restore my pursuit of wholesome influences.

Personal Coaching Questions

Developing the
Art of Friendship

1. In what ways have I noticed an improving quality emerge within my friendships?

2. What can I note as constituting this change?

3. In what ways have I even "raised the bar of expectation" within my personal friendships?

4. What criteria do I use in evaluating my relationships, current and future?

Reflection 39

Noticing the Apparent

The fog on top of the mountain where I live in northern Alabama this morning is so thickly layered like one silk pillow stacked so beautifully atop another. I notice that all I can see is that which is closely apparent, with the dense fog preventing my view beyond. I can see the stone flower garden next to my house, but beyond that, everything else is blocked from view. I think, "The flowers in the garden are so lively with the cool mountain air and the dew, causing their colors and beauty to illuminate against the grayness of the day." Parallels to thoughts about life, in general, are everywhere in this. Many times, the big things come along in our lives, pulling our focus and effort away from that which is so beautifully close to us! Hence, the fog settles in and, in a providential way, seemingly blocks from view that which exists beyond us at the moment. With this narrowing of our view, we see the things that are so closely apparent, but are so often missed in exchange for the broader view. I wonder, "Shouldn't the things more close to me be consistently maintained and delicately manicured since these are the things always with me?"

Personal Coaching Questions

Noticing the Apparent

1. Am I prone to noticing the "closely apparent," or am I more of a "big picture person," being less concerned with the fine details present within life's experiences?

2. Have I noticed lately that my attention has been drawn away from the important things, like family, the beauty of nature, or the value of solitude? If so, does this represent a shifting trend that I might need to address in my life? What changes might I make in order to correct this trend?

3. Have I noticed my schedule to be more erratic of late? Does my schedule lend itself to more contemplation time or less so?

4. What things might I implement in order to correct the problem before it becomes a crisis?

Reflection 40

Charting Life's Process

As I view the cliffs and chasms in the mountains of northern Alabama this morning, I am, in the same moments, retracing the emotions of my most recent life journey. The tough experiences of life appeared to be filled with seeming impassable chasms at the time. Looking back, I survived the rough journey by God's rich grace. Today, with my mind enlarged, I stand upon the highest peak of my life ever scaled, and looking down upon the chasms below, they appear as mere trenches in the vast terrain traveled. The view from where I now stand is remarkably breathtaking!

Personal Coaching Questions

Charting Life's Process

1. Describe a recent spiritual, personal, or life experience journey.

2. Charting one's life's process is best achieved over a significant period of time. The keeping of a running reflective journal provides a wonderful evaluative tool for future assessment, blessings and enjoyment in the process of the journey. Where in the charting of this journey do I see myself at this present moment?

3. Where do I see myself in the future? What is my plan for getting there? List in detail.

4. What strategies might I adopt that reveal my future efforts to put these plans in action? List in detail. Future journal entries might consider the ongoing development of and commitment to these strategies from this point forward.

"If I never live to see my name attributed to any accomplishments of significant notoriety, I trust that I can merely model in my latter days how one should truly enjoy, in the simplest yet most pleasing fashion, the life one has left."

David Dalton